MW01241212

Reprinted by permission, the McKinley Pub. Co.

MAP OF NORTH AMERICA

Approximate locations of places from which archaeological vegetal material has been sent to the Ethnobotanical Laboratory for study, and upon which determinations have been returned during the period covered by the report.

OCCASIONAL CONTRIBUTIONS FROM THE MUSEUM OF
ANTHROPOLOGY OF THE UNIVERSITY OF MICHIGAN
NO. 1

THE ETHNOBOTANICAL LABORATORY

at the

University of Michigan

BY

MELVIN R. GILMORE

ANN ARBOR, MICHIGAN
UNIVERSITY OF MICHIGAN PRESS
June 7, 1932

ISBN (print): 978-1-949098-62-4
ISBN (ebook): 978-1-951538-62-0

Browse all of our books at
sites.lsa.umich.edu/archaeology-books.

Order our books from the University of Michigan
Press at www.press.umich.edu.

For permissions, questions, or manuscript queries,
contact Museum publications by email at umma-
pubs@umich.edu or visit the Museum website at
lsa.umich.edu/ummaa.

ADVERTISEMENT

The publications of the Museum of Anthropology, University of Michigan, are made through the medium of a single series — the Occasional Contributions. The individual papers constituting the series are issued at irregular intervals as opportunity permits.

The Occasional Contributions are numbered serially, in the chronological order of their separate publication. When a sufficient number of pages have been printed to make a volume, a title page, index, and table of contents will be supplied to libraries on the mailing list for the series.

The subject matter of the individual contributions prepared by staff members and friends of the Museum includes descriptions of museum collections and field work, results of research, and discussions of field and museum techniques.

Carl E. Guthe
Director
Museum of Anthropology
University of Michigan

TABLE OF CONTENTS

THE ETHNOBOTANICAL LABORATORY AT THE UNIVERSITY OF MICHIGAN

ACKNOWLEDGMENTS

THE reader may be interested to know how the Ethnobotanical Laboratory had its inception. In the summer of 1930 several archaeologists requested me to make botanical identification of miscellaneous vegetal materials which they had recovered from field operations in various archaeological sites. I very willingly complied with the requests, for I have long held the belief that as careful study should be made of all vegetal remains of prehistoric human cultures as of any other criteria of culture. In my view the development of a people's phytotechnic is fundamental to the development of all their arts of life.

After complying with some of these requests, I talked with Dr. Carl E. Guthe, Director of the Museum of Anthropology, discussing with him the work that had been done, and forecasting the possibilities and the importance which the work might have in the forms of evidence it would bring to bear in judgment of vanished cultures. Dr. Guthe was quick to see the potential value and significance of the work. As chairman of the Committee for State Archaeological Surveys of The National Research Council he suggested sending out a general invitation to archaeologists to send in any archaeological vegetal material they might wish to have identified. I was quite agreeable to the undertaking, the invitation was sent out, and soon material from all over the country began to come in with requests for its identification.

Happily in recent years the feeling of exclusiveness among workers in fields of scientific investigation has given way to a tendency toward coöperation. This more generous attitude accrues to the common advantage of all and to the greater advancement of science.

The existence and usefulness of the Ethnobotanical Laboratory depend upon the helpfulness of many different persons and institutions. First of all the Laboratory could not have had its beginning but for the favorable and helpful attitude of the Director of the Museum of Anthropology, Dr. Carl E. Guthe, and of the University Administration in authorizing the facilities requisite to the work.

I wish to acknowledge my sense of great indebtedness to the members of the University Herbarium staff for their unvarying kindness and for frequent use of the herbarium collections. My thanks are due also to staff members of the School of Forestry and Conservation, and of the College of Pharmacy, to Dr. J. H. Kearney and Mrs. Agnes Chase of the Bureau of Plant Industry, U. S. Dept. of Agriculture, to Dr. L. H. Bailey, Ithaca, New York, and to Mr. George F. Will, Bismarck, North Dakota.

Without the interest and coöperation of archaeologists and ethnologists in the field there would be no material for study in the Laboratory. For the opportunity of examining archaeological vegetal material from their collections I have to thank the following persons: Miss Katharine Bartlett, Museum of Northern Arizona, Flagstaff, Arizona; Mr. Charles E. Brown, Historical Museum, State Historical Society, Madison, Wisconsin; Prof. E. F. Castetter, University of New Mexico, Albuquerque, New Mexico; Mrs. Mary Russell F. Colton, Museum of Northern Arizona, Flagstaff, Arizona; Prof. S. C. Dellinger, University of Arkansas, Fayetteville, Arkansas; Mr. Thorne Deuel, University of Chicago, Chicago, Illinois; Mr. Robert Goslin, State Museum, Columbus, Ohio; Mr. M. R. Harrington, Southwest Museum, Los Angeles, California; Mr. E. B. Howard, University of Pennsylvania Museum, Philadelphia, Pennsylvania; Mr. Horace Jones, Rice County Historical Society, Lyons, Kansas; Dr. A. V. Kidder, Carnegie Institution, Washington, D. C.; Mr. T. C. McMahon, Detroit, Michigan; Mr. Frank Mitalsky, Phoenix, Arizona; Mr. Earl H. Morris, Carnegie Institution of Washington, Washington, D. C.; Mr. P. H. Nesbitt, Logan Museum, Beloit College, Beloit, Wisconsin; Mr. Jesse Nusbaum, Laboratory of Anthropology, Santa Fe, New Mexico; Mr. William Ritchie, Rochester Museum of Arts and Sciences, Rochester, New York; Mr. H. C. Shetrone, State Museum, Columbus, Ohio; Dr. Wm. Duncan Strong, University of Nebraska, Lincoln, Nebraska (now Ethnologist, Staff of Bureau of American Ethnology, Washington, D. C.); Dr. Alfred M. Tozzer, Dept. of Anthropology, Harvard University, Cambridge, Massachusetts; Prof. W. S. Webb, University of Kentucky, Lexington, Kentucky.

THE IMPORTANCE OF ETHNOBOTANICAL
INVESTIGATION[1]

THERE is one division of ethnological investigation which has ever been sadly neglected. I refer to ethnobotanical inquiry and collection. It is strange indeed the neglect should have occurred, for the relation of a people, especially of a primitive people, to their floral environment is obviously fundamental to all their culture. This consideration is of the utmost importance for a clear understanding and a fair appraisal of economic conditions and of traits of material culture.

A primitive people live well or ill according to the wealth of useful species of plants at their disposal. Primitive tribes, such as our Indians, depend immediately upon the floral environment first of all for food; not only for their vegetal food, which is a very considerable part of their fare, but also ultimately for such animal food as they have, for the animal life in any region depends in both quantity and quality upon the plant life.

Under such conditions of intimate dependence upon the vegetation of their habitat a people would naturally be induced to become acquainted with all the plants which grew about them, and which held so large a practical interest in their lives.

The first and most urgent demand of man, as of every other living creature, is for food. Besides food, man requires shelter and clothing against the inclemencies of the weather. He needs also a considerable variety of materials from the plant kingdom for use in the manufacture of tools, implements, weapons, utensils, and other conveniences useful in

[1] Published in *Am. Anthrop.* 34 (No. 2): 320-325. Reprinted here with adaptations.

the acquisition, transportation, storage, and preparation of the materials required for these prime necessities.

After these requirements have been met, man has always and everywhere sought the satisfaction of aesthetic desires. He requires not only materials for utilitarian uses, but those which are able to give pleasure: ornament in clothing, embellishment of furnishing in habitation, and objects pleasing to the eye in symmetry of form and color. Pleasing odors in clothing and in places of abode are desired, so perfumes are sought; rhythmical and melodic sounds are needed to please the ear or to compose the mind in religious rituals, so musical instruments are made. For illness or injury medicaments and instruments are required.

To supply the means of satisfaction of all these demands very thorough exploration has been made by every tribe of the vegetal resources of its region. Not only has tribute been exacted from all forms of vegetation in the respective regions, but importations have been made from surprising distances of useful vegetal products not indigenous.

Interpretation of Culture Traits

The study of ethnobotany is of very great importance for the aid it gives to a proper understanding of the interrelations of all the several traits and of the whole material and intellectual culture of a people in its entirety. The study often will throw a clear illumination upon matters of tribal economics, of politics, of custom, of religious ritual, ceremony and symbolism, and other traits of culture which might otherwise be unintelligible or at best ambiguous. Without the light afforded by ethnobotany a researcher may easily go far astray and make a sorry misinterpretation of his observations. I am reminded of the interpretation given by a very eminent anthropologist to a common saying which was current among the people of a certain Indian tribe, viz., there was a saying in the tribe to the effect that wild flowers should not be plucked because they contain the souls of little

children. He regarded this saying as the statement of a
peculiar tribal belief in regard to human souls. To me it
immediately suggested the teaching which I have heard
among all the tribes of my acquaintance upon the sanctity
of all life, and specifically as to conservation of plant life.
Indian children were taught by their parents and elders that
plants and animals must not be needlessly killed, that wan-
ton destruction is wicked. A precept frequently heard was:
"Do not needlessly destroy the flowers on the prairies or in
the woods. If the flowers be plucked, then there will be no
flower children (seeds); and if there be no flower children,
then in time there will be no people of the flower nation
(plant species). And if the flower nations should thus die
out of the world, then the earth would be sad. All the
flower people, and all the different nations of living things
have their own proper place in the world, and without them
the world would be incomplete and imperfect."

I think it was similar teaching which was heard by the
eminent anthropologist I have mentioned; because he knew
nothing of the intimate relation of the people to their floral
environment, nor of their habits of thought with reference
to vegetation, and because he was himself quite unaccustomed
to think about plants, he entirely misconstrued the meaning
of the people in the saying which he heard quoted.

Ethnobotanical study not only prevents misapprehension
and misrepresentation of the significance of observed facts,
but it is positively necessary in very many instances to the
correct diagnosis and explication of ethnological facts, of the
symbolism of objects used, and the significance of allusions
in the text embodied in ceremonial ritual. When it is recorded that at a certain stage of the ceremony "a wisp of
grass" was used in a certain manner we have no clue to the
significance which the act had for the celebrants nor even
any certainty that it was grass, much less what species. It
may have been actually not a grass but a sedge, or some
other plant even more remote from relationship to any of

the grasses. We need to know exactly the species of plant used in any given ceremony, for as a matter of fact, in any such case it was strictly prescribed for the given ritual. In each such prescription the given species was required because of its symbolic meaning and of its psychologic bearing in the mind of the people.

The esoteric meaning of a ceremony in which plants are employed cannot be grasped unless the species and the reaction of the tribesman's mind to the species is known with certainty. In the Indian thinking with reference to plants each species has its own proper function in the constitution and working of the world. It is because of these several functions of the various species that, for example, different particular species of plants are used by Indians as incense in different ceremonies, the various incenses being burned for particular purposes. Therefore, when the observation is made of the use of an incense in a ceremony, we must know specifically what that incense is so that we may know just what is the idea or train of thought implied in the act. Ethnobotanical study gives us an illuminating line of evidence upon the ethnic psychology and the rationale of tribal rites and religious ceremonies.

As a Measure of Culture

By a knowledge of the relations of a people to the indigenous vegetation of their own region, and that of other regions near or farther away we have a means of measuring their cultural status, and their contacts with other peoples. We may gain knowledge of their agriculture, if agriculture was practised, and much of the pattern of their customs and habits of life. We may learn of ancient commerce and commercial routes. By the evidence of ethnobotany the centers of domestication and the lines of distribution of cultivated species may be determined. We may obtain suggestions for additional uses of plants besides those now employed by our own people; we may also learn of useful qualities of other species not now cultivated, which might profitably be domesticated and improved by selective breeding and cultivation.

Relation to Symbolism, Ceremonials, Philosophy, Linguistics, History

It is not only the tribal economic botany, interesting and useful as it may be, which we should seek. A proper ethno-botanical study of any people would include much more than this. We should make inquiry not only into the Indian economic botany, uses of plant products for food, food accessories, manufacture of cordage and textiles, tools, implements and utensils, habitations, furnishings and fixtures, perfumes, dyestuffs, and other uses; but we should make inquiry into the whole range of knowledge of plants and plant life. So fundamental to the aboriginal life of every tribe of Indians were their relations to plants, so complete was the ramification of these relations, that a competent consideration of ethnobotanical facts in a proposed study of any tribe is essential to any fair and adequate presentation of every phase of the study; neglect of such consideration can result only in an incomplete and probably misleading presentation.

Only by the inclusion of an ethnobotanical study of a people can we form a full and fair representation of their material and mental culture. Such study is necessary in order to gain an understanding of much of their folklore, their phenologic observations and the dating of seasonal industrial activities, and of festive and religious occasions, ritualistic forms and symbolism, allusions in myths and legends, their geographic place names, and new words in vocabularies of languages changing gradually during the long course of migration into new regions. An example of this last category might be mentioned in the instance of the origin of the Dakota word *ti^{n}psi^{n}na*, for the plant the scientific name of which is *Psoralea esculenta*.

The following explanation of the name *ti*ⁿ*psi*ⁿ*na* has been offered by Dr. J. R. Walker, formerly physician at the Pine Ridge Agency, and a careful student of Teton-Dakota ethnology. Before the immigration of the Teton-Dakota into the Plains their abode had been in the region of the western Great Lakes and the head waters of the Mississippi River. In that region one of their most important articles of food was the grain of wild rice, *Zizania aquatica* L. Their name for this plant is *psi*ⁿ. When they moved into the Plains region they no longer found *psi*ⁿ. In the new home another important food plant was found which in a manner compensated this lack. The new food plant was *Psoralea esculenta* Pursh, a legume having a farinaceous root which furnished a large measure of very palatable and nutritious food. The Dakota word for prairie is *ti*ⁿ*to*ⁿ. The new food found on the *ti*ⁿ*to*ⁿ, hitherto unknown and therefore unnamed must have a name. Nothing appeared more fitting than to call it the *psi*ⁿ of the *ti*ⁿ*to*ⁿ. This name could be expressed in a term compounded from *ti*ⁿ*to*ⁿ, prairie, *psi*ⁿ, wild rice, and *na*, the common diminutive suffix often used as the termination of plant names in the Dakota language. In the composition of this word signifying "the prairie *psi*ⁿ," or "the *ti*ⁿ*to*ⁿ *psi*ⁿ," the ultimate syllable of the word *ti*ⁿ*to*ⁿ is elided and we have *ti*ⁿ*psi*ⁿ*na*.

It might not be thought that the findings of ethnobotanical inquiry would be necessary or even useful to linguistic studies, but the foregoing and the following instance will show that they may well be so. The very earliest flower to appear in spring on all the northern prairies is the blossom of the Pasque Flower, *Anemone patens* L., var. *wolfgangiana* (Bess.) Koch. The name of this flower in the Dakota language is *hokši-čekpa wahča*, which means "twin flower," *hokši-čekpa* being the word for twin, and *wahča* the word for flower. Why the flower should be called "twin flower" by the Dakota is not self-evident, but the explanation of the reason is an interesting fact in Dakota psychology and

Dakota plant nomenclature as it is in Dakota linguistics. This flower is the first of all to bloom; appearing while the weather is still cold, many times it is covered by the later snowfalls, but it comes through and shows its cheerful blossoms amid the snow. Because it is the first herald of returning spring it is regarded with peculiar affection by all the people of the regions in which it abounds, and its coming is eagerly expected. The Dakota liken the feeling which greets the appearance of it, the first-comer of spring flowers, to that feeling of fondness and glad expectancy which awaits the birth of the first-born child of a human family. So they call this first spring flower the "twin flower," linking it thus with the first-born child of a family. The child and the flower are counted twins in the fond, yearning hope which awaits their coming.

Scope of Primitive Science

I have said before that it is not Indian economic botany only which we should seek. The economic botany of a people is very interesting and useful, but it is after all only a part of the science of botany. The whole scope of a people's knowledge of the science should be explored. We should learn what their naturalists know about plant anatomy, of the plant as a living organism, and its parts, and the terminology they use. We should learn what they know of plant physiology, of the organs of plants, and their functions. We should obtain their views of plant taxonomy and their methods in nomenclature. We should learn what they know of plant ecology, the relation of plants to their environment and their powers of adaptation, and of association of species. We should also find out what they know of phytogeography. Among tribes practising agriculture we should inquire into their knowledge of phytoculture, of amelioration and acclimatization.

It will be seen that adequate exploration of the ethnobotany of a tribe is in itself no slight task. However much or little of such information it is possible to obtain, it is all very helpful to other lines of ethnological and archaeological investigation. In every archaeological exploration the greatest care should be exercised to preserve every trace of vegetal remains, whether carbonized or in exsiccated condition. From such vegetal remains we may obtain important evidence in regard to the distribution of species of plants in prehistoric time, and of their former uses and of degrees of advancement in technique. Also, in the instance of cultivated plants, we should thus find the evidence of lines of distribution of crop species and of the stages of advancement in the improvement of such species. From the material we might also learn much concerning routes of travel and commerce, and of the commodities exchanged in such commerce.

THE ORGANIZATION OF THE
ETHNOBOTANICAL LABORATORY[2]

THE Museum of Anthropology at the University of Michigan in 1930 entered upon a new departure in the establishment of an ethnobotanical laboratory. It is the purpose of the Laboratory to examine archaeological and ethnological materials of vegetal origin to determine their botanical identification as to species, and to interpret their human uses or significance. To this end it was intended to build up at the Laboratory collections of such materials as extensive and comprehensive as possible.

Through the Committee on State Archaeological Surveys of the National Research Council an invitation was extended to archaeologists throughout the country to submit specimens of all materials of vegetal origin which they might recover in the course of field work, together with data as to place, time, and circumstances of discovery. After the specimens were examined and studied at the Laboratory they were to be returned to the senders if desired, with statements as to their botanical identification and their uses and significance in the life of the people in whose culture they were associated. It is greatly to be desired that the Laboratory may be allowed to retain any duplicate specimens or surplus materials in its permanent collections, where the proper records will be made of them, and they will be catalogued and made available for the use of students.

The collections of the Laboratory as classified and catalogued are to be filed in units which are designed in multiple sizes fitted into trays within dust-proof cabinets. Within the units the materials are placed in various sorts of containers

---

[2] This paper was delivered at the Anthropological Section of the A. A. A. S. in Cleveland, December, 1930.

according to their nature. Much of the material from archaeological exploration is in carbonized state resulting from the action of fire which destroyed the structures in which it had reposed. Other materials have been preserved by complete dessication in moisture-proof caves and rock shelters. These materials include fragments of structural material of habitations and other buildings, fragments of utensils, implements and tools, fabrics woven from vegetal fibers, articles of attire, objects of ceremonial use, and plant products used medicinally. The containers vary to fit the requirements of form and volume of the materials, but all containers conform to the unitary system of the Museum of Anthropology. The compartments of the storage units are made in standard dimensions, each an exact multiple of the next smaller container, so that there is the utmost economy of space and the most complete order of arrangement and system. There is the greatest degree of facility of access to specimens by reference to the index. The more bulky specimens are disposed in cartons of unitary sizes to accommodate in the most compact manner the varying requirements of cubic space, and to facilitate examination at any time. Specimens of finer material, such as seeds either carbonized or in natural condition, are disposed in glass phials closed by cork-lined metal screw caps. The phials are of uniform sizes fitting in numerical sets in the smaller sizes of cartons. It will be seen that the plan is intended to make all the material of the Laboratory readily available for examination, and the location and withdrawal of a specimen for study as simple as the drawing of a book from the shelves of a library.

The response accorded to this invitation of the Laboratory at the University of Michigan, by individuals and institutions in the archaeological field has been very encouraging. Specimens have been received from a number of places over a wide area of the Southwest, and from the East, the South, and the Central and Western regions. Determinations upon these specimens have been furnished to the inquirers, and in almost every instance the Laboratory has been permitted to retain the specimen.

It is confidently expected that the service of the Laboratory as an exchange and clearing house of information, and as a special museum of objective study material in archaeology and ethnology, will be of signal benefit to science. It is intended not to duplicate but to supplement the service of such instrumentalities as are afforded at present by various herbaria in this and other universities, botanical gardens, and the National Museum, and to give more immediate facility for convenience of special students, and to interpret the material in the light of the information possessed by the curator in the results of his ethnobotanical researches among Indians of historic time in their bearings upon archaeological questions. The significance of ethnobotanical researches among Indians of historic time is of tremendous importance for the light such research throws upon the relations between prehistoric peoples and their floral environments. Customary and habitual use of certain plants for food and food accessories, medicines, perfumes, dyes, fabrics, etc., may be traced in many cases directly from cultures of contemporary time back into prehistoric cultures. The relations between primitive man and his physical environment, the soil, climate, flora and fauna of his habitat are intensely vital.

Man's customs, habits, manner of living, his specialization of occupations, division of labor, differentiation or lack of differentiation of social classes, rituals of religion, instruments of government, in fact all that makes up his cultural complex is conditioned in large measure by the flora and fauna of his habitat. Therefore it is extremely important to study the relation existent between a tribe and its physical environment in order to understand its cultural pattern.

Even very cursory consideration of the several culture areas of the continent of North America will reveal the close correlation existing between them and the floral provinces of the continent. It will be seen that the several culture areas are delimited by lines which closely coincide with the lines of demarcation of the floral provinces. It should be quite evident that no clear understanding of the evolution of cultural traits can be had nor any true interpretation of their significance made without considering them in relation to the environment amid which they had their origin, together with the impacts they have undergone from the environments into which these traits have become diffused.

Long experience in gathering ethnobotanical information from living Indians of various tribes in different parts of North America makes it possible for me to give interpretation of the cultural significance of the large part of archaeological vegetal remains which is not obvious. Many uses and processes of phytotechnology among Indians of historic time trace back in unbroken continuity to remote prehistoric time.

When sufficient evidence has been accumulated in the form of vegetal remains from archaeological exploration, and the evidence thus acquired has been charted on maps and diagrams, it will be found a source of much aid in tracing the chronological and geographical distribution of cultural traits. From the stores of wild harvests and from stores of agricultural crops when present, from structural material of habitations, and from materials used in attire, in fashioning of tools, implements, and other utilities, much significant information can be obtained.

Maps and diagrams such as I have mentioned will be illuminating in tracing the range of certain types of corn, of squashes and pumpkins, and of beans, sunflowers, and other crops cultivated by prehistoric peoples, and more will be learned concerning the diffusion of these crops. It is conceivable that such evidence might go far in the determination of centers of domestication of certain crop plants.

Some evidence already has been found to indicate the incipient stages of cultivation of certain species of plants which were later abandoned, and of the prehistoric dissemi nation and extension of range by human agency of some native uncultivated species. Archaeobotanical evidence will also give some information on the relative times of appearance of certain traits in prehistoric cultures. For example, from the evidence of vegetal remains it appears that while the Ozark Bluff Dwellers were far advanced in the cultivation of types and varieties of corn, beans, sunflowers, and both squashes and pumpkins, yet they did not possess the bow, nor did they have tobacco.

Besides the collection of archaeological material it is purposed to build up in the Laboratory a collection of material for comparative study in identification of archaeological vegetal material. This comparative, or check collection should comprise a great diversity of seeds, roots, tubers, bulbs, stems, barks, fibers, and all parts and products of known species of native plants. The collection of products of known species will then serve for matching and identifying the unknown products recovered from archaeological exploration. Such a collection of comparative material is necessary for our purpose for the reason that an ordinary botanical herbarium is inadequate. The ordinary herbarium is good as far as it goes, but the botanical herbarium is designed for a different purpose and is frequently found deficient in some essential features for matching vegetal products and materials from archaeological remains. It may often occur that an ethnological or archaeological specimen of vegetal origin may be made from parts of a certain plant which would not ordinarily appear in a good botanical herbarium specimen of that same species of plant. Our comparative collection therefore should be an herbarium, but also more than merely an herbarium.

The Laboratory, with its collections and its records, will provide a clearing house of information in the fields of ethnology and archaeology upon the relation of primitive cultures to their floral environments, and will also be a special museum of vegetal material obtained in archaeological and ethnological exploration. Opportunity is offered to archaeologists and ethnologists throughout the country to have their materials of vegetal origin botanically identified and ethnologically interpreted.

The importance of this work may be appreciated when it is realized that all the elements which make up the cultural complex of a people are conditioned in large measure by the factors of their physical environment. This conditioning applies not only to the features of material culture, but also to the traits of mental culture, to habits of thought, figures of speech, unwritten literature, imagination, ritual and ceremony, and customs. It should be plainly manifest that the origin and persistence and the variation of cultural traits such as social and political institutions, myths, and ceremonials and rituals can never be rightly understood, nor can any true interpretation of their significance be made, unless their relations to the geographical and biological environment in which they had their origin, together with the modifying effects they have undergone from other environments which they have encountered in the course of their diffusion, are taken into consideration.

SOME RESULTS OF THE FIRST YEAR'S
OPERATION OF THE ETHNOBOTANICAL
LABORATORY[3]

IN PREVIOUS pages of this paper something was told of the aims and purposes of the Laboratory and its proposed methods. I now intend to show some of the results of the work during the first year of operation and to indicate some of the developments which may be expected in the future.

Specimens have been submitted from archaeological exploration of sites in southern Nevada, Arizona, New Mexico, Colorado, Texas, Kansas, Nebraska, Arkansas, Illinois, Kentucky, Ohio, and New York. These specimens to the number of several hundred, have been examined and studied by me, and reports rendered to the archaeologists who have submitted the material; copies have been filed also in the records of the Laboratory. In most instances, the Laboratory has been permitted to retain the specimens, as they are from duplicate or surplus material in the collections of the explorers. In this way a considerable collection of archaeological vegetal material, together with the findings upon its study, is being accumulated which will continually increase in quantity and in scientific value for regional and chronological comparative study.

Whether the specimens be retained in the collections of the Laboratory or returned to the consignors, at all events the archaeological explorer is made acquainted with whatever information his specimens have yielded, and at the same time the sum of all such information is classified and filed in the records of the Laboratory where it is available for researchers. More and more as various facts accumulate in these records they will fall into their proper order and se-

---

[3] The substance of this paper was read at the Anthropological Section of the A. A. A. S. in New Orleans, December, 1931.

quence to link up the parts and chapters of the archaeological story of the continent so far as the relation of human cultures to plants is concerned, and that relation will finally be found to be no small part of the story.

Everywhere in the world the relation of human kind to the indigenous flora has been intimate and intense, not only from the immediate connection of certain species with the needs and activities of man in numerous ways, but also mediately through the relation of certain other species of plants to the indigenous animals which in turn have greater or less effect upon man's thoughts and actions, ways of living, food habits, clothing, daily occupations, and social organization. The geographic influences, the physical environment encompassing human life in a given region, most profoundly modify the trend of racial habits and inherited tendencies in the mental and material cultures of human groups. Unless the physical environment within which a complex of cultural traits has taken form can be visualized, it can never be understood how and why that complex has arrived at a particular pattern.

To look at some of the materials which have been sent to the Laboratory for identification may prove of value. The work of examining and identifying archaeological specimens of vegetal origin is trying. It requires agility and versatility of mind, fertile scientific imagination, close application, attentive and critical observation, and ready and comprehensive correlation of widely diverse facts.

The technique of the work varies according to the great variety of materials. The specimens may be of wood, bark, fiber, roots, rhizomes, tubers, bulbs, stems, leaves, flowers, fruits, nuts, resins, fungi, or of deformed and hypertrophied growths. These materials may have been preserved from decay by dessication in situations impervious to moisture, or they may be in a charred condition to which they were reduced by the action of fire.

The technician who would determine the identity of plant species to which the materials belong must possess a good knowledge of the anatomy of a wide diversity of plants, and recognize under unusual conditions plant parts and botanical species. He must also have good knowledge of phytogeography. All this may be of no avail without a considerable knowledge of ethnic economic botany, for it is from this source that the technician will discover clues for his guidance to comparative study material by which to match, and thus to identify, the unknown specimens.

A consideration of some of the material which has come into the Laboratory will illustrate my meaning. A quantity of charred seeds has been received from a site in southwestern Colorado. The question is: From what species of plant are they derived? First they are examined visually. They appear to be seeds of some plant of the family Compositae. Species of seeds in that great plant family that might have been stored by Indians as these were stored are considered. It may be they were to be used for food. Among the possibilities that come to mind from my knowledge of such uses, a knowledge gained first hand from living Indians, is the seed of wild sunflowers, *Helianthus annuus*. The specimen is compared with known specimens of *Helianthus annuus* from the comparative study collection, and they are found to be matched. The material has been identified.

An example may be given of material consisting of charred fragments of rhizomes. These specimens also were found in a village site in southwestern Colorado. From a knowledge of plants used and valued by living Indians, a clue is sought to the possible species of these rhizomes treasured for some use by a vanished people whose domicile in the Colorado River region was destroyed by fire many centuries ago. By reason of what is known of uses of plants by Indians of the present day, a plant is thought of whose rhizomes resemble the specimens in question, and which Indians hold in extraordinarily high esteem for medicinal and ceremonial uses, that is, sweet flag, *Acorus calamus*. *Acorus calamus* does not grow in the region where the specimens were found. It is known, however, that prepared products of it could have been imported there if it were highly valued and a sufficient demand existed. A comparison of the unknown specimens with known specimens of *Acorus calamus* rhizomes shows that they agree in every particular feature of their structure. Thus the specimens are identified and at the same time it is learned that at the archaeological horizon which they represent, there was commerce which drew products from as far away at least as eastern Oklahoma, for there is no point nearer, even at the present time, where *Acorus calamus* is found growing.

Another group of specimens consists of some charred blades and culms of a species of grass from a site in Kentucky. They have been recovered from the ruins of a prehistoric clay wattled house destroyed by fire. By comparison it is decided that they are the big bluestem grass, *Andropogon furcatus*. From my work with living Indians I have learned that it was this same species of grass which was used by the Pawnee, the Arikara, the Omaha, and other tribes of the Missouri River region in the construction of earth covered houses, and for lining storage pits in which corn and other crops were stored underground. They used this species of grass for the purpose because, unlike other species, it is not attacked by mould when in contact with earth. It was, doubtless, for the same reason that it was used for tempering the clay wattling by prehistoric people of Kentucky.

The Laboratory contains specimens of the same species of grass from the lining of underground storage pits in archaeological sites in New York and from caves in Ohio, as well as from remains of Ozark Bluff Dwellers. Thus the uses of this grass as found in modern ethnological investigation, appear, from the evidence of the specimens, to have been discovered in remote archaeological time, and to have contin-

ued from the Plains west of the Mississippi all across the
continent as far eastward as the range of the species extends.

From a Pawnee site in southern Nebraska, a quantity of
seeds of some chenopodiaceous plant has been secured.
These seeds are 3 mm. in diameter, but there is no species
of chenopodium, or any nearly related plant indigenous to
that region having seeds more than 1 mm. in diameter. The
seeds in the specimen resemble more nearly than any others
the seeds of *Chenopodium nuttalliae* Safford, a species of
chenopodium which was cultivated as a grain food by the
Aztecs, and still is cultivated in Mexico for that purpose.
Now the question arises: Was this Aztec species of chenopodium also cultivated by the Pawnees in Nebraska at the time
this village was occupied? If it was formerly cultivated
by the Pawnees, why was it not reported by early travelers
who did mention the Pawnees' crops of corn, beans, pumpkins, and squashes? The answer may well be that these
travelers, who knew little and cared less about the culture
of the Indians, may have seen but did not recognize this
plant as a cultivated crop. They would, from previous acquaintance and long association, recognize corn, beans, and
squashes; but a field of chenopodium would probably appear
to be an abandoned field overgrown with weeds.

This archaeological find causes me to wonder if perhaps
some other crops besides corn, beans, and squashes were
brought from Mexico as far as Nebraska by the Arikaras
and Pawnees, but which have since been lost along with
other cultural losses caused by the invasion of the white
race.

Considerable quantities of seeds of the giant ragweed,
Ambrosia trifida, were found among other vegetal remains
in dry rock shelters in the Ozarks. These seeds were much
larger in size than those of the species which now grows
as a weed without care. They are also of a uniformly light
color, whereas the seeds of this species growing as a weed
are quite variable in color, some light and some almost

black. In studying the possible and probable uses of this plant by the prehistoric Bluff Dwellers, I thought of the eagerness with which its seeds are sought by birds. I gathered a quantity of fresh newly ripened seeds to try their suitability for human food. I found them of good flavor and apparently rich in food value. From this quality in the fresh seeds and from the select appearance of the specimens discovered in the stores laid up by the ancient Bluff Dwellers, I concluded that the plant was probably cultivated by them as a grain crop for food.

In sites of the Ozark Bluff Dwellers there have been found stores of seeds of *Iva ciliata*. These seeds also are of larger size than seeds of the species now growing as a weed. This fact, together with the fact that large quantities were stored by the Ozark Bluff Dwellers, and that such care was taken of them, suggests that this plant also may have been cultivated by those people although it has never been found in cultivation by any tribe in modern time. Whether cultivated or not it seems to have been greatly valued for some purpose. It might have been used for food, but the rather striking odor would seem to preclude such use. The distinct but pleasing odor would suggest its possible use in medicine. Inquiring among Indians, I learned from Arikaras of North Dakota that they have heard of this plant being used medicinally by some southern tribe, but on this point they have no definite information. The Arikaras, however, also say that their own people use, or formerly used, the young and tender plant as greens; they say it "tastes like string beans."

The behavior of both these species of plants indicates a considerable antiquity of human association and habituation to man's activities upon the soil, for although if the plants ever were cultivated they have since been repudiated, their cultivation abandoned, and they have been driven out from man's protection, still they show their preference for the vicinity of man's abode by hovering about grounds which

have been disturbed by man's activities, but which have
fallen into neglect.

In connection with the discussion of *Ambrosia trifida*
it may be of interest to say that a specimen from the Ozark
Bluff Dwellers is a fragment of a screen made from the stems
of this plant woven with a warp of twined fibers.

Among other materials recovered from a dry cave in
Ohio are quantities of fibers of *Apocynum cannabinum* some
of which are in the form of raw material; some of the fibers
have been manufactured into twine and thread and woven
into fish net.   One specimen of the fiber was found which
revealed, as had not been known before, a method of the
first preparation of the raw material in the field where gathered, making a great saving in the matter of transportation,
an item of no small moment when all transportation was by
human carriage.   The specimen shows that the woody part
of the plant was roughly hackled out and the fibers loosely
twisted into hanks, probably near the place where the stalks
were gathered, thus greatly reducing the bulk and weight for
transportation home.

From a dry cave in the Ozarks, a fragment of the peculiar down woven blanket has been received.   Examining this
closely, I found that in this instance the material from which
the web is woven consisted of yarn twined from the fibers of
Apocynum cannabinum on which the down was wound.   Examining the down, I found it to be that of wild ducklings
which had not yet grown feathers.   The down was not
plucked, but strips of the duckling skins were wound spi-
rally, down side out, upon the fiber twine.   When I saw
how this was done, I at once correlated this fact with the
method of taking waterfowl which was practised by prehistoric Indians and continued down to present time, and which
I have personally witnessed.   Young waterfowl, not yet
feathered, and adults in moulting, while still unable to fly
from the lack of plumage, were run down and captured by
hand.   Although the weaving of vegetal twine and duckling

down blankets has stopped since white traders have brought woolen blankets, the art of twining native fibers has still persisted in some degree to the present time, and I have witnessed its practice. So in this, and in many other instances, ancient and prehistoric activities and industries can be interpreted by the light of knowledge gained from living Indians of their uses of indigenous resources.

The tepary, *Phaseolus acutifolius*, is indigenous in the Upper Sonoran life zone from western Texas to southwestern Arizona, and is now also in cultivation throughout the Southwest. The common garden bean, *Phaseolus vulgaris*, had its origin in Central America and appears to be with maize, which also had its origin in the same region, a member of the aboriginal American agricultural complex. Now since both these species of *Phaseolus* are cultivated throughout the Southwest the question arises of priority of one or other of these species in the agriculture of that region. By examination of the earliest agricultural remains from the Basket Makers it is found that they cultivated *Phaseolus vulgaris*, but not the native *Phaseolus acutifolius*, at least there is no evidence of that species from their remains. Recently, however, there came to the Laboratory a specimen of *Phaseolus acutifolius* from a site of Pueblo II culture in northern Arizona. This is the earliest specimen of this species known to me.

It appears, therefore, that the idea of agriculture, its technique, and the first seed stock were importations from the south, having their origin in Central America. Once the idea and the practice of agriculture had taken hold in our Southwest, trial was made of some of the species native in the region. Thus, the tepary bean, *Phaseolus acutifolius*, and perhaps the sunflower, *Helianthus annuus*, were there brought into domestication, probably long subsequent to the earliest cultivation of *Zea mays* and *Phaseolus vulgaris* in their original center. At all events there is good evidence of the cultivation of the sunflower by the Ozark Bluff Dwellers in specimens of cultivated sunflowers from that culture which are as large as any of our modern sunflowers. Up to the present time these specimens of sunflowers from the Ozark Bluff Dwellers are the earliest evidence there is of the cultivation of this plant, a species which is indigenous from the Rio Grande to western Canada throughout the Plains.

An interesting and significant bit of evidence of the care given by Indian agriculturists to the selection and maintenance of pure strains in plant breeding was found in two specimens, one from the culture of the Ozark Bluff Dwellers and the other from the crop of the Hopi of the year 1931. From the crop of the Hopi was obtained an ethnological specimen, a pumpkin of the species *Cucurbita moschata*. The Hopi said it was from their own ancient stock. Shortly after the receipt of this specimen from the Hopi there came to the Laboratory a piece of pumpkin rind from a site of the Ozark Bluff Dwellers. This specimen exactly matched in texture and color pattern the specimen of pumpkin cultivated at the present day by the Hopi.

Another bit of similar evidence was found in a specimen of one variety of *Phaseolus vulgaris* from a site of Pueblo II in Arizona which was matched by a specimen of one of the varieties of *Phaseolus vulgaris* grown at the present time by the Arikara in North Dakota, and which they have carried with them through centuries of migration from the borders of Mexico to their present location on the upper Missouri River.

In the remains of the Ozark Bluff Dwellers there was found an ear of yellow dent corn eight and one-half inches in length, having twelve rows of grains on a red cob; that is, it is quite similar to the present day yellow dent corn of the great Corn Belt region whose original seed stock was obtained from the Indians of Virginia by the first English colonists.

As the range of territory from which specimens are re-covered becomes more extensive and study of the material more intensive there will be more light upon the centers of origin, the lines of procession, the succession and increases in number of agricultural varieties of cultivated species, and the advancement of the peripheral bounds of the entire agricultural area.

From these studies it is also hoped to gain many points on borrowing of cultural traits, and to learn much of prehis-toric commodities and trade routes. In all these and in many other ways, ethnobotanical research may become very fruitful in measures of assistance to both archaeology and ethnology.

INSTRUCTIONS TO ANTHROPOLOGICAL FIELD WORKERS

Concerning Ethnological Data[4]

BOTANICAL OBSERVATION IN CONNECTION WITH PURSUIT OF OTHER LINES OF INVESTIGATION

IT IS not to be desired that an investigator of Indian linguistics, folklore, material culture, social organization, religious ceremonies, tribal law, or other special ethnological topics, should turn aside to make inquiry in regard to Indian botany. It is not to be expected that he could pursue this special inquiry to equal advantage with one who is botanically trained; but it is desirable to have every field worker in any special ethnological province alert to the possibilities of tribal plant lore impinging upon his own special field. He should be able to sense these correlations when they exist, and he should be able to follow their lead and to take advantage of them to the enrichment of his own special study. The most favorable arrangement would be that of coöperation of the workers in several lines of ethnological investigation through which each one would profit by the stimulus and extended horizon afforded by the views of the others. The point of view and inquiries of the botanist would bring out additional facts and discover new implications of phenomena already observed which otherwise would never appear.

METHODS

Every investigator, when in his own particular quest he comes upon any sort of reference to a plant or to a vegetal product should make note of it and should make certain the identification of the species. He should not fail to record carefully the name of the plant in the language of the tribe studied, and he should secure an identifiable specimen for

---

[4] Published in *Am. Anthrop.* 34 (No. 2): 325-327. Reprinted here with adaptations.

record. This specimen should be certainly identified by the Indian informant and should later be specifically identified by a systematic botanist. For example, if the investigator is inquiring about basketry or matting or cordage he should obtain as a part of his record botanically identifiable specimens of the plants used in these manufactures. If dyes are used for decorative designs on these fabrics the sources of the dyes should be ascertained and specimens obtained of the plants furnishing the dyestuffs.

If an item is learned on the use of certain seeds for making beads, or on the use of perfumes for the hair or clothing, or concerning symbolic objects used in religious ritual, then the identification of the plant from which these products are obtained should be made sure by securing specimens of the plants themselves.

The investigator should bear in mind that actual observation, fully and carefully recorded, accompanied by a specimen or specimens identified by the Indian informant, is worth more than any hearsay or second-hand information. Such records and specimens are of permanent and inestimable value in many and often unexpected ways.

The field worker in ethnology may desire some instruction as to materials to be secured, and methods for their preservation, together with the items of information to be sought. In the first place he needs to know how herbarium specimens are prepared and preserved. The standard size of herbarium mounting sheets is 11½ by 16½ inches, so all dried specimens of plants should be within this size limit. If a specimen be larger it may be bent while still flexible, before it becomes stiff and fragile by drying. In the case of trees and shrubs, branches representative of the whole plant may be used.

An herbarium specimen should consist of all characteristic parts of a plant, not only those above ground, including buds, leaves, flowers, and fruits, but also underground parts, such as roots, rootstocks, and tubers, or other distinguishing parts. Usually a single specimen could not be made to show all these parts, but two or more specimens collected at different times might well be secured.

PREPARATION OF SPECIMENS FOR HERBARIUM

To prepare specimens each should be laid out flat with leaves and flowers extended between sheets of absorbent paper. The specimens, thus one above another on a board or other flat surface, should have another board laid over all and pressure applied by a weight or by buckled straps or tied cords. The pressure should be sufficient to prevent leaves or flowers from wrinkling in drying, but not so great as to crush any tender parts. For absorbent sheets one may use blotting paper, carpet paper, or even old newspapers folded flat and smooth. The drying papers should be changed every day until the specimens are completely cured.

SPECIMENS OF PLANT PRODUCTS

Besides herbarium specimens for identification of the species it is desirable also to collect specimens showing Indian utilization of the plant. For this purpose specimens of raw materials should be prepared showing the stages of preparation through which they pass, and also specimens of the finished product. Various receptacles suited to the various natures of the materials may be used to contain the specimens; the receptacles may be tough paper bags or boxes, muslin bags, glass jars and phials, tin boxes, or cans. Each specimen should be carefully and securely labeled, for specimens are useless without proper data. Each specimen should be marked with a number, and the numbers should correspond to the chronologic order in collecting. Each number should be entered on a data sheet or in a note book; full information concerning the specimen which is marked with the corresponding number should be appended. The data sheets may be made in some such order as follows:

1. Number	7. Name of tribe from which the information was obtained
2. Blank space for insertion of botanical name when determined.	
	8. Name of Indian informant
3. Blank for name of botanist who identified the specimen	9. Uses of the plant
	10. Parts used
4. Common or popular English name of the plant	11. Place where information was obtained
5. Name in language of the tribe and etymological analysis of this name	12. Date of collecting
	13. Name of collector
6. Tribal name of any product made from this plant	14. Remarks

DISCRIMINATION AND CAREFUL SIFTING OF INFORMATION

Under "Remarks," very full and detailed description may be given, the fuller the better; all details should be entered at the time the observation is made or the information obtained, and never left to memory for any later entry. Moreover, the statements should be verified at the time by review with the informant in all particulars. This review should be most thorough, so that if the observer has erred or has misunderstood the informant, or if the informant has misunderstood the query in the first instance such errors may be corrected.

If any plants which are not indigenous to North America are noted as used by Indians, mention should be made of the fact that they have been introduced and that therefore they are not of aboriginal Indian use, but their use has probably been learned from the white people. It is very confusing to the reader if plants which have been introduced from Europe and have escaped and become naturalized in America are listed without discrimination among plants which are indigenous. In some instances Indians no doubt have learned uses of these introduced plants from their white neighbors. If unqualified statements are made by observers that such plants were used by Indians the statements are quite misleading. In a proper ethnological study of any tribe of Indians the items comprised in the aboriginal culture should be clearly differentiated from those borrowed from other sources.

DISTINCTION BETWEEN INDIGENOUS AND INTRODUCED PLANTS

I make particular mention of the distinction between indigenous and introduced plants because I have in mind certain papers published under titles claiming for them that they are "The Ethnobotany of the . . . . Indians." Several papers have appeared with similar titles, under the names of several different tribes. In these papers a considerable number of plants introduced from Europe have been listed as having Indian uses, and no intimation is given that they are not indigenous to America, and so, of course, could not have been used by or known to the Indians before the coming of the white men. The lists include burdock, catnip, coltsfoot, camomile, dandelion, ground ivy, lamb's-quarters, mullein, mustard, peppermint, shepherd's purse, velvet weed, wild parsnip, and other plants which are not indigenous, but no indication is given to the reader that such species are not native to America, indeed the inference is left that they are native. In these papers uses of these foreign plants by Indians, which must have been learned from white people, are given in the same manner as aboriginal uses of indigenous plants, leaving the reader in ignorance of the mixture of European acculturation elements with the elements of aboriginal culture. Such confusion is deplorable. In any proper and competent ethnological study of an Indian tribe an attempt should be made to learn not only the items of borrowing, or at least of learning by whites from Indians, but those items which Indians have learned from whites and have adopted for their own use should also be noted.

ETYMOLOGY OF INDIAN PLANT NAMES

Careful record should be made of the etymological analysis of the names of plants and of botanical terminology in the language of the tribe studied. Reference has been made already to the importance of this rule. Such etymological evidence may disclose significant facts not otherwise discoverable.

It is hoped that this discussion may be in some degree helpful to all ethnological field workers, and it is offered in order to suggest a means of acquiring a more ample and adequate body of information in the cultural study of any tribe, and an additional instrumentality to aid in a clearer and more definitive exposition of tribal culture and further security against error and misinterpretation of observed actions and appearances.

CONCERNING ARCHAEOLOGICAL DATA

When vegetal material recovered from archaeological explorations is sent to the Laboratory for identification and record it should be accompanied by a letter giving as full information as possible. A serial number should be securely attached to each object. In the accompanying sheet of information the several objects should be listed by their serial numbers and information concerning each should be given. After the identifying number a general description of the object should be given. If a number of sites have been explored the number of the site in which the object was found should follow. The geographical site should be indicated with sufficient accuracy upon a map accompanying the information sheet, or by the land description numbers of the Congressional Survey, or by other geographical definition, or by both map and description.

It would be well to give according to the maps and charts of the United States Biological Survey the life zone in which the site occurs. It would be an advantage to record the ecological situation, whether it be forest, grassland, or

SUGGESTED FORM FOR INFORMATION SHEET ACCOMPANYING
ARCHAEOLOGICAL SPECIMENS

Date sent	Condition of material
Sent by	Biological life zone of site
Date collected	Floral formation of region
Where collected	Plant association of site
Location of site	Reference to publication
Archaeological Period	Description
Stratigraphic position	

desert shrub, and to follow that with the dominant vegetation association, e.g., oak-hickory, beech-maple, oak-pine, or other woodland association, or the bluestem sod, bluestem bunch grass, or other grassland association, as it may be.

The culture period of the site should be given as nearly as may be determined, for example, Basket Maker II, Pueblo I, Pueblo III. The time in the period should be given. As full information as possible should be given concerning conditions and circumstances under which the specimen was found. Under this head come details concerning the soil or other material in which the specimen was embedded.

The foregoing items are needed for proper identification of the specimens; the latter items are useful as indicators of conditions of life under which the people lived and of the activities carried on by them. A knowledge of conditions and circumstances surrounding the recovery of the objects is very helpful in a critical consideration of their significance. For example, in a site of the Ozark Bluff Dwellers two peach pits were found. At once an explanation is demanded as to the means by which these specimens could have been intruded there, for the peach is not indigenous to North America. It is an introduction from the Eastern Hemisphere, ultimately from the far Orient. When the conditions of this site and the conditions of the find are known it becomes evident that signs of recent work of rodents are present.

The explanation of the presence of this specimen among materials of a prehistoric culture is that it was intrusively deposited by the agency of rodents in recent time, perhaps from the remains of the lunch of some picnic party. From another site of the Ozark Bluff Dwellers came a single fragment of a peanut shell. The peanut is originally from South America, and is not known in pre-Columbian time farther north than Mexico, so this specimen was also probably introduced by a rodent into the site where it was found.

A specimen of seeds was sent in from a site in northern Arizona which had been determined as of the archaeological period of Pueblo II, a period closing more than a thousand years ago. The seeds were found to be of the Western Yellow Pine, *Pinus ponderosa*. When tested in the laboratory they were found to be viable. The viability of the seeds showed conclusively that they had not reposed for a thousand years in the situation where they were found, that they could have been there no long time, and probably had been deposited there within the past year. Inquiry in regard to the conditions developed the information that the site where they were found was in a cave and that in this cave a great many nests of pack rats were found.

From such instances as these cited it should be clearly seen that it is important to note carefully all the conditions of the situation in which specimens are found. It should be noted if a roadway passes near the site, if there are modern habitations, fields, gardens, or orchards near by, if any recent work of rodents or other animals is evident, if there is any appearance of disturbance of the earlier by any later human culture, and if there are any other circumstances which might have a bearing on findings at the site. It is also important to note the nature of the immediate terrain, the physiography of the immediate region, the nature of the local flora, and the facilities of communication with neighboring and more distant regions.

It is important to note the stratigraphic position in which the specimen was found, and its association with a certain type of habitation or pottery or fabric which would be diagnostic of the culture level existent at the time when and place where the specimen was deposited. By such evidence it may be possible to establish the first appearance and successive stages of advancement in the cultivation of any given species of plant. Thus it may be discovered when and where began the process of domestication and amelioration of those species of plants not included in the primal complex of cultivated plants of the Western Hemisphere, the later accretions, such as tobacco, some of which, such as teparies and sunflowers, were adopted far from the original center of American agriculture.

Something should be said here as to the packing of archaeological vegetal material for safety in transit. It must be remembered that all this material is extremely fragile. Much of it was, even in its original and best state, flimsy and easily shattered, and centuries of exsiccation have made it still more frangible. Those vegetal specimens which have been charred by fire are often extremely brittle. The greatest care must be used in packing such material in order to prevent destruction by the stresses caused by jarring, shaking, and rubbing during transit. All such fragile material should be well wrapped in cotton, tissue paper, or other soft substances, and packed in shredded paper or fine excelsior, all firmly bedded in a box, crate, or carton in such manner that there can be no movement of material within the package. If movement is possible among the individual pieces within the package, they are sure to be damaged by attrition. If a little care is taken in the packing, according to the instructions here given, the most delicate and fragile material can be securely transported without damage.

Made in the USA
Middletown, DE
14 May 2023

30535923R00027